Pub date Feb 24

POPE PIUS XII

POPE PIUS XII

PRIEST AND STATESMAN

A Biography
by
KEES VAN HOEK

Foreword by
THE MOST REV. DR. BROWNE
Bishop of Galway

PHILOSOPHICAL LIBRARY
NEW YORK

Nihil Obstat:

JOANNES BURKE,
Censor Theol. deput. Dublinensis.

die 19 Novembris, 1939.

To
I. R. A. W. WEENINK
Netherlands Consul-General in Dublin
A PROTESTANT OF UNFAILING SYMPATHY AND
UNDERSTANDING FOR THE CATHOLIC NATION
TO WHICH HE IS ACCREDITED

Foreword

The historian describes the events and person-
ages of the past: it is the art of the journalist to
seize the meaning of contemporary happenings
and to describe for us the men who are directing
the course of the events amid which we live.

Mr. Kees van Hoek has shown all the power
of a great journalist in this life of His Holiness
Pope Pius XII. He has given a full, accurate
and vivid description of the man and his remark-
able career, from a delicate boy in Rome to be
supreme ruler of the Catholic World. His description of Eugenio Pacelli is all the more in-
teresting because of the intimate and personal
touches with which it abounds—a most impressive
picture of the personality of the Pope, the majesty
of his appearance, the charm of his manner and
the aroma of holiness that surrounds him.

This is none of the superficial flippant write-
ups of the sensation-loving Press, but a carefully
drawn. sincere portrait by one who has the power
to recognize and depict greatness — greatness of
character and of ideal.

For the author reveals to us not merely what

manner of man Pius XII is, but also what kind of work he is trying to do for this sad world. He shows us the mind of the Pope from his letters and his first Encyclical as summed up in his device, "The work of Justice is Peace." Pius XII works for Peace, but he reminds the world that there can be true peace only when there is Justice; and there is Justice only when Christ reigns in the hearts and counsels of men.

Here is the true leader of the Christian world who will restore mankind to the path of true human welfare and progress. Over against the figures of those 'leaders' whose power rests on brute force and whose policies lead necessarily to war and destruction, there rises up in the world of to-day one figure, that of Pius XII. He represents the principles of humanity, of universal brotherhood, of justice and civilization, for he is the representative in this world of the only foundation of these values — the cornerstone Christ. He is the only world leader who is above all territorial ambitions and political prejudices, and he has this other unique qualification — he knows the world. Literally he knows the world, for he has travelled and met men of all nations and can speak to them in their own language. He knows how they feel, their hopes and fears, their possibilities and limitations. He is too good a European to fall into the calamitous mistake of imposing on peoples a

4

system for which they have neither liking nor aptitude. He sees beneath the surface of political institutions down to the realities. He has sympathy with all peoples. It is only such a man who can apply the principles of justice to the tangled web of international interests and disputes.

If the world is ever to be restored to the way of sanity and peace, it will need a Peacemaker, a man in whose justice and wisdom all can trust. Pius XII is the Peacemaker whom God has raised up for this world, for God has endowed him with justice and wisdom beyond the measure of mortal ken. If the world is to be saved from destruction it must turn to Pius XII and hearken to him.

But first of all we of the Catholic Church must turn to him in all loyalty and confidence, realizing what manner of man Providence has raised up to be our Supreme Pastor, what extraordinary gifts and powers have been given him for the fulfilling of his great office.

The Christian peoples of the world must insist now that the Governments which profess to fight for justice and Christian civilization shall not repeat the tragic and criminal intrigue of the London Treaty of 1915, whereby anti-clerical influence excluded the Pope from the Peace Conference Table. The world has paid a terrible price for that vile bargain with Irreligion. To-day every country realizes that peace and justice are spiritual

5

realities, dependent on a spiritual foundation.
They cannot be applied to — or secured in — this
world of ours without the intervention of that
Power which alone has authority from God to
interpret and to expound His Law.

✠ MICHAEL BROWNE,
Bishop of Galway

CONTENTS

POPE PIUS XII

I

THE GREAT EXAMPLE

EARLY on a warm morning in August, 1938, charabancs unloaded the faithful by the hundreds at the village of Castel Gandolfo, like a swarm. By noon the dreamy little square and the narrow streets adjoining were jammed with the private cars of tourists turned pilgrims for the day. Even Geneva in its heyday could not have mustered such an array of international number plates: expensive " GB's " between spotless Dutch " NL's " and light French " F's " ; " Chicago, Ill.", hobnobbing with the " Ciudad de Buenos Aires." For in this out-of-the-way village in the Alban mountains the aged Pope Pius XI spent the summer, and twice a week he reserved a morning for public audiences. Perched on the highest vantage point, like the medieval castle which it is, the Villa Papale dominates the countryside. The unruffled Lake of Albano, with a colour like the patina of copper, dreams at its feet, between the wooded slopes, a jewel set in the midst of sun-scorched hills.

We waited in the main audience chamber. Gradually this vast marble hall got packed tighter and tighter, with the steady overflow from the other salons which lined the Pope's way from his private apartments. Before the red velvet and gilded throne stood a microphone, and underneath busily humming and swirling electric fans, tall Swiss Guards, with sun-bronzed faces, pikes in hand, their breeches and vests of broad yellow and blue stripes with red, making a vivid splash of colour.

As the hour advanced courtiers came hurrying by in their gold embroidered uniforms, busy Monsignori, their purple mantillas trailing behind, officers of the Papal Guards in stiff round lace collars—as if they had just stepped out of an old picture of cavaliers. Already the windows near the throne had been shut, to forestall draughts, but the waiting seemed endless. This, verily, was a slight sample of eternity! Irish brogued with the Middle West; Bologna hailed Saragossa; squat, dusky airmen from San Salvador jabbered round tiny aloof Chinese; a towering negro, blacker than his black cassock, stood near a group of fair and athletic German youngsters in shorts and sports shirts. Here we all waited, sprung from every nation and race, come from over every one of the seven seas.

Suddenly, from behind the closed doors, a clapping broke loose. It galvanised each of us back from weariness into tense expectation. The doors swung open and the clapping swelled to a tremendous crescendo as the Pope came into view, carried past a group of seminarists in the adjoining room, now evoking a tumult of cheering as sturdy hands lifted his chair to the level of his waiting throne.

He was already a man at death's door. Eighty-one years old, having carried the burden of the Papacy for over sixteen years, he had won by sheer tenacity his first round with death a year before. Hardening arteries, a weak heart, bad circulation—this was the trouble. "Just an old man," a doctor had summed it up with pathetic resignation. Just an old man—but one who was not allowed to relax from the heaviest burden which mortal man can bear, for he held the conscience of some hundreds of millions of Catholics in liege. And that in an epoch of growing State totalitarianism, in which he was more and more looked upon as the visible head of Christendom, defending eternal values against modern onslaughts.

The Pope sat down heavily. Behind him, immobile, stood the officers of his Noble Guard, aristocratic faces frozen under golden helmets, martial chests covered with decorations. The Pope shuffled his painful leg into a position of some comfort on the cushion for which he had asked below his breath. The dark eyes behind his rimless spectacles roamed the hall, his tongue swallowed laboriously. The close atmosphere of this hot day with all its people was stifling at the tail end of a busy morning ; he had been up since six, as was his wont, been receiving since nine, and it was now well past one.

An old man, indeed—but what energy ! His fingers drummed on his chair, for the cheering did not show any abating. Though his entourage tried to stem it, it was of no avail against such long pent-up enthusiasm. Until he himself took the matter in hand ! A short and decided gesture, as if he literally cut the cheering off, sharply and resolutely. A hush fell which in its suddenness was almost uncanny. Behind his spectacles a light flickered up, the beginning of a smile broke round that weary mouth. And a

12   (D 1132)

warm, soft voice commenced almost shyly :
"You would have clapped me into eternity." . . .
Everyone seemed to realize the bitter-sweet word-
play, for a moistness crept into many eyes.

I scanned the thousands of faces lifted up to
him. Curiosity had turned into affection, with
even the most blasé of them. But on those of
the faithful, for whom he was the Vicar of Christ
on earth, spread the reflection of their inner
vision, and complete filial devotion. It seemed
as if their intense eagerness had conveyed the
meaning of his opening sentence even to those
who did not understand the language in which it
was uttered. And as I listened to the music, not
so much of what he said, as of how he said it—
giving himself so completely in his slow, soft-
spoken homily, underlining here and there a
special point, with an insisting twist of the hand,
his little mannerism, pausing now and then, his
sturdy hand fingering the pectoral cross, as if
choosing deliberately the only word to fit—I
thought of his long and busy life . . . his birth
of small people, near Milan, at a time when the
Austrians still ruled Lombardy . . . his brilliant
studies and his return as head of the Ambrosian
Library, the Bodleian of Italy. From there he
was transferred to the Vatican, later to become

B

Nuncio to Poland, in the hectic years at the end of the war. He returned home, once more, this time as Cardinal Archbishop of Milan, to be elected some six months later, in February, 1922, as Supreme Pontiff, two hundred and sixtieth in succession of St. Peter, whose Fisherman's ring he now wore.

Cardinal Achille Ratti had taken the name of Pius as a pledge of peace. But the conciliation with the Italian State was to remain the only great peaceful achievement of his Pontificate. It became, instead, his lot to wage incessant battle against the encroachment of the absolute State over individual and family. He had to rule with a strong and sure hand, for he stood in the middle of every conflict and of every problem, though he had wished, himself, for no other life than that of the scholar. How he delighted everyone when he spoke at Merton, in 1914, at the unveiling of Oxford's statue to Roger Bacon.

It was nearing two o'clock before he had finished. As if the Pope had drawn fresh vigour, he rose to give his Benediction, alert, standing erect and firm, almost thrust forward, as with a clear voice he invoked the blessing of the Father, the Son, and the Holy Ghost, making

14

the Sign of the Cross with wide sweeping movements, lingering over it as if he implanted it on everyone individually.

An ovation followed. The German " *Heil, Heil, Heil* " boomed like heavy guns amidst the rapid clatter of the Italian " *Eviva's.* " I had seen Pius XI leaving St. Peter's in the zenith of his reign, carried high above the faithful in the Sedia Gestatoria, with the triple crown on his head, white ostrich feathers fanning behind his jewel-studded cope, silver trumpets announcing to the hundreds of thousands on the Piazza his triumphal entry on the balcony. But it was this leave-taking which will remain unforgettable. The old, tired and yet so powerful face, the hand which trembled in the waving of a good-bye which was half blessing and tenderness, half imperious command.

He was to have his lunch, his siesta and his drive through the gardens, and then, from five until midnight, he would sit in his study, signing decisions and nominations, reading reports, preparing for his encounters of the morrow. Only a light supper, served on a tray, broke the second day into which this man of eighty-one regularly turned his evenings. He used to retire at the stroke of midnight some hours after he had dismissed his household. But he always extinguished his lamp a little while before, to look out over the silent lake and the dark mountains. He had been born in a little town from which he could see the snow-covered Alpine ranges : they had been his earliest passion. Some of the riskiest records in mountain climbing stood to his name. Gazing at the serenity of the peaceful Alban hills, slumbering underneath their canopy of stars, he thought of his wondrous night watches amidst snow-capped giants. For he was a mountaineer by right of conquest, and the exhilaration of a day well spent never waned, not even in this closing year of his great and brave life. . . .

Some months afterwards, shortly before Christmas, he overcame another severe sinking with superhuman courage. On February 11th, 1939, he was to receive all the Italian Bishops on the occasion of the Twelfth Anniversary of the Conciliation between the Church and the State. The way things had deteriorated after Hitler's visit to Rome—during which the Pontiff had left the Eternal City in protest against the " Crooked Cross," the Swastika—the racial laws against the Italian Jews which had followed in its wake, the increasing paganism of the radical wing of the Fascist Party which was constantly gain-

ing ground, had disquieted the Pope profoundly.
He was not the man to shirk his duty, and with
eager interest the world was anticipating his
allocution to the Italian Episcopate. He had
been working on it for days, deep into the nights.
Knowing the poverty of so many bishops of small
country dioceses, he had envelopes prepared with
everyone's name and a thousand lire note placed
in each, to defray travelling expenses, asking for
Masses for his intention.

That Allocution was never to be delivered. At
the very last moment, during the night between
February 9th and 10th, his condition suddenly
grew worse. He died, as he had always wanted
to, in harness, but a few hours after he had left
his desk, where he had been occupied with his
great task. His last words were "Jesus, Italy,
Peace."

II

ELECTION

A SLIM, tall and dark dignitary in the vivid
crimson of a Cardinal bent over the dead Pontiff.
He was Eugenio Pacelli, as Secretary of State
long his closest collaborator, as Camerlengo of
the Church highest in dignity after the Pope,
who, now that the throne of St. Peter had
become vacant, took charge.

Pius XI was dead, and a whole world mourned.

On the day of his burial, walking from Fleet
Street to Westminster, one saw the Union Jack
lowered on the Law Courts, the Australian, New
Zealand, and South African colours from the
offices of their High Commissioners, whilst from
the Admiralty and all the Government Departments in Whitehall flags also flew half-mast.
Never had the British Nation thus honoured a
dead Pope, but this one had personified peace
and decency against bullying and war mongering.

" Never," to quote Mr. Duff Cooper in the

ELECTION

London *Evening Standard*, " since the Reformation, had the election of a new Pontiff been awaited with so much anxiety by the whole world." The Anglican Archbishop of York was one of the many non-Catholic religious leaders who asked his flock " to pray for God's guidance in the election of a new head for the greatest community in Christendom."

For that election every Cardinal had gone to Rome ; not a single one was absent through distance or infirmity. They gathered in conclave at the Vatican, severed from every connection with the outer world. Filing into the Sistine Chapel, they made, on their thrones alongside the walls, a living purple frieze underneath Michelangelo's " Creation." They were all there : the Cardinals from Turin, Milano, Naples and Venice ; from Munich, Cologne, and Vienna ; from Prague, Warsaw, and Budapest ; from Westminster, Paris, Toledo, and Lisbon ; from Antioch, Malines, and Armagh ; from Boston, Philadelphia, and Chicago ; from Rio de Janeiro, Buenos Aires, and Quebec—sixty-two in all. Solemnly each one left his throne in turn, his long scarlet robes trailing over the thick carpet as, holding his ballot paper, he knelt before the Altar reciting aloud his solemn oath : " I take Christ

19

the Lord who will judge me as witness, that I
have voted for him of whom I believe before God
that he must be elected,'' dropping his ballot
paper in the golden chalice.

An absolute majority of two-thirds being
necessary, Papal Conclaves have been known to
last for days. This one proved to be one of the
shortest in history. After the ballot, the voting
papers were unsealed, called out by the
scrutineers and checked on printed lists on the
green covered desks before the thrones of the
Cardinals. After the third ballot on that historic
March 2nd, 1939, it was uninterruptedly the
name of Eugenio Pacelli which echoed through
the sacred hall. Forty, forty-one, forty-two—
the two-thirds majority had been passed, but the
counting of his name went on until it had reached
sixty-one of the sixty-two votes. Long before
the last vote was recorded, Cardinal Pacelli had
stopped checking up on his own list; he had
realized what he felt as a dreadful truth; his
hands were tightly clasped together and his eyes
were shut. He kept his head high, but his face
was so pale as to be almost livid. The last vote
had been registered; all but he himself had
voted for him—a unique happening, of which in
two thousand years of Church History there is

hardly another example, just as only twice before, in the sixteen hundreds, a Secretary of State had been elected to succeed as Pope. By an electric device the canopies above all but one throne were lowered. The Cardinals left their seats and gathered round their Dean, who asked the elected if he accepted. Barely audibly, Pacelli replied, " Since it seems God's will, I accept, and I take the name of Pius XII." Then one by one the Cardinals, who only a minute before had been his equals, knelt before him, kissed his right foot as a token of obeisance and embraced him with the kiss of peace.

Outside, an enormous crowd filled St. Peter's Square, the vastest in the world, linked to the Cathedral by the classic colonnades of Bernini with their hundreds of stately marble columns. It is the custom that at an inconclusive vote the ballot papers are burned with some moist straw, and the dark smoke thus emitting shows the outside world that no majority has yet been reached. Twice that day the dark smoke had gone up, until at 5.30 in the afternoon a thundering roar of joy greeted the thin white spiral, followed by the announcement of the Cardinal Dean from the balcony of the name and title of the new Pope. When the bells of the 365 churches of the

Eternal City began to toll their triumphant
message, tens of thousands hurried to join the
hundred thousand already gathered on the
Piazza. Dusk had begun to fall when at 6.20 in
the evening of his sixty-third birthday a deathly
pale, tall figure, wearing his white silk robes for
the first time, appeared on the open loggia outside St. Peter's, to intone with a steady voice the
invocation for his first papal benediction, *urbi et
orbi*—to the City and to the World. The world,
which he knew as few Pontiffs before, universally
acclaimed his election—from the " reverent
homage " of Mussolini to the " true happiness "
expressed by President Roosevelt. Rome
especially acclaimed him with spontaneous
fervour, for the new Pope, it had not happened
for two centuries, is a Roman of the Romans.

III

THE ROMAN

THE new Pontiff hails from Ponte, a quiet quarter of the City of Rome near the river Tiber. One can see the Dome of St. Peter's from there and the Angel on the Castle of the Caesars. In one of its sedate streets, the Via degli Orsini, stands the Palazzo Pediconi—a big four-storied house, stuccoed a reddish brown, unassuming as Roman *palazzi* go, a high gate leading to a small court-yard with its bubbling fountain, that soothing sound which is so typically Roman and different from the exuberance of other Southern cities. The old rubs shoulders with the new even in this street off the beaten track ; there is a modest Madonna statue at the corner of the house, never without its small votive light or a few flowers, but the ground floor wall is bedecked with modern posters, advertising olive oil and radio.

On March 2nd, 1876, in the third storey, a dark-eyed boy was born, carried round that very same day to the neighbouring baroque parish church of San Celso, where his uncle baptized him Eugenio Maria Giuseppe Giovanni. The names themselves indicate a pious family, for they invoked on their Eugenio the protection of St. Mary, St. Joseph, and of St. John, the beloved Disciple. That boy was destined to become the 261st successor of St. Peter as Pope of Rome.

The family, small country aristocracy, originally hailed from the province of Viterbo. An uncle, Cardinal Catterini, had called Marcantonio Pacelli, the grandfather of the present Pope, to Rome, and had supervised his juridical studies. Later, Cardinal Antonelli, Prime Minister of the then Papal States, made him Under-Secretary of State for the Interior. In 1870, when Victor Emmanuel of Savoy became first King of a United Italy, Marcantonio Pacelli refused the invitation of the new Italian Government to become a Royal Councillor of State. His loyalty remained pledged to his own Sovereign, the aged and ever-forbearing Pio Nono, who had become voluntarily a prisoner in his own palace; that loyalty he kept until his death at the age of a hundred.

Of his seven sons one became a famous banker,

founder of the " Banco di Roma " ; the third, Filippo, a prominent politician, one of the leaders of the " Unione Romano," the clerical party. By profession he was Dean of the Consistorial Advocates, the Vatican Bar, whose members one sees at pontifical ceremonies in their old Spanish court dress of carmine red and black velvet. He had married the Hon. Virginia Graziosi, who came from one of the old Patrician families of Rome ; their union was blessed with two sons and two daughters. The eldest, Francesco, followed his father's career. He was the lawyer who, in intimate collaboration with Pius XI and the Duce, did most of the labour which resulted in the historic Lateran Treaty of 1928, whereby the Papal See and the Italian Kingdom composed the differences which had rent Church and State so deeply that even the aristocracy of Rome was divided into a " Black " section, stubbornly loyal to the Pope as Sovereign, and a " Red " accepting the King. On the day the Treaty was signed the two brothers Pacelli—Francesco, the lawyer, created a Marquis for his services, and Eugenio, then already Archbishop and Nuncio— decked the grave of their parents with flowers, to celebrate the conciliation of the two Romes.

Eugenio grew up as most boys of his surround-

ings did. He played " Mass " in the little chapel
he had made at home, as so many Catholic boys
do the world over, deadly serious. As a young
child the tales of the missionaries set his imagina-
tion on fire, and he came home to tell his mother
that he wanted to become a missionary, too,
" but without the martyrdom," he added
cautiously.

Orthodox though the Pacelli family were, this
was, nevertheless, blended with a certain matter-
of-factness. For a boy of a Catholic home to
attend a State school was almost unheard of in
these days. Yet Eugenio was sent to the
Visconti Grammar School because his father
considered that it had then no equal in
Rome. The clash of opinions and sentiments
strengthened his convictions. Once the boys
were told to write an essay on a " Maker of
History," and one of his class-mates had chosen
St. Augustine as his subject. The history master
ridiculed the choice in front of the class. Eugenio
stood up and took the blame ; it had been his
advice which had induced this choice, and as
for himself he was quite willing, if the master
allowed, to defend it there and then. When he
left the Grammar School, matriculating with
honours, he not only had the best mark for

languages, but was awarded the gold medal for history. One of his teachers, Professor Antonio Neviani, to this day recollects him as a model pupil, " serious, studious and intellectually outstanding."

It had been expected that he would enter the legal profession, but reticent Eugenio nursed the hope of studying for the priesthood. That he felt as a vocation ; notwithstanding the occasional banter of his friends, he liked to go in the quiet of an evening to a church to pray and meditate. Finally, being allowed to enter the Capricana Seminary, he had to leave it after a year, the rigours of community life were too dangerous for his delicate health. He had grown too fast for his age, a tall, gaunt youth. His health began to fail alarmingly ; medical opinion prescribed a complete rest, but soon found out that his studies, to which he clung with all his heart, should not be denied to him. His father's influence with the Ecclesiastical Authorities secured him the unusual experience of remaining in the midst of his family whilst engaged in his study for the priesthood. He went daily to the courses of the Capricana, following all the same, at home, the observances to which he would have been subject as a resident student. Only every morning, on the orders of the doctor, he went for a canter on horseback through the Roman Campagna, over those roads bordered by tall pines and olive orchards, roads full of the remains of ancient times, the grand aqueduct on his way out, the spires and cupolas of the city his vista on his way back. Here his love for nature, for the simple people, and for the city of his birth was born.

The summer holidays he spent on the family estate, where as a boy he had followed his father after hares and partridges. Punctual in the extreme, it was Pacelli's modest boast that he had never been late or kept anyone waiting, save in one instance which he is fond of recounting. To reach Rome from their country place, he had to go by carriage to Orvieto, the nearest railway station. Scalabretta, the local coachman, used to stop half-way, at San Lorenzo, for a drink. As he was fond of his horse, he used to give it a pint of wine, too. One day when young Pacelli was suddenly summoned to Rome, he drove down to Orvieto Station himself. Passing San Lorenzo the horse stopped and expectantly turned round for his usual pint. Pacelli remembered, and told the inn-keeper to make it two pints this time as he was in a hurry and wanted

28   (D 1132)

the horse to feel its very best. Indeed, the Rosinante took the next hill in great style, but having reached the crest he found such an exertion too exhausting and lay down for a quiet snooze. Pacelli had to walk the rest of the way— it was his first experience of the wisdom of moderation.

IV

GASPARRI'S PUPIL

ON Easter Sunday, 1899, after having been ordained Priest by the Patriarch of Antioch the day before, he said his first Mass in a side chapel of the great Basilica of Santa Maria Maggiore. The memento picture which he gave to friends and relations present begins: " Eugenio Pacelli Romanus "—the Roman. His typical Roman features, the high, clear forehead and the classical round eyebrows in the perfect oval of his face, shone with emotion. To have become a priest, for which he was destined by birth and been trained by choice, meant the realisation of his deepest calling. Deeply pious, thoroughly schooled, his faith was a synthesis of knowledge and sentiment. His fondest wish was to become a curate. But destiny willed otherwise.

One day when he was at home playing his beloved violin to his sister's piano accompaniment, a caller was announced—Monsignor

Gasparri, the Secretary of the Congregation for Extraordinary Ecclesiastical Affairs, the first department of the Papal Secretariate of State. The young aristocrat respectfully kissed the sturdy peasant hand of his high visitor. Pietro Gasparri, the later Cardinal-Secretary of State of two Popes, whom Mussolini has described as the greatest diplomat he ever met, was a giant by stature. He came from a mountain village in the Abruzzi, and with his relations, simple peasants, he chatted of local births and deaths, harvest and sheep-shearing. His way was to take the bull by the horns, and he had set his mind on getting this young brilliant priest in his office. Pacelli demurred : he had hoped for a parish. But Gasparri boomed his loud laugh : '' So you want to become a shepherd, but I want you to become a sheep-dog to shy away the wolves,'' and as Gasparri had a way of winning the day, Pacelli became first an *apprendista* or junior clerk, soon a *minutante* or principal copyist in Gasparri's department.

That was in 1901. Leo XIII was still on the Papal Throne, and that *Grand Seigneur*, Cardinal Rampolla del Tindaro, his Secretary of State. Forty picked clerics were employed in this most important Vatican State Office,

31

housed on the top floor of the Vatican palace,
from where the development of ecclesiastical
affairs in all countries of the world was closely
watched. Going through all ranks, Pacelli
quickly reached the Under-Secretaryship. Such
was his reputation that once, when there was a
deadlock in some delicate negotiations between
the French Government and the Holy See,
Gasparri finally said to the French Ambassador,
Hanotaux, " This must be cleared up, I'll send
you my best man, young Pacelli " ; who promptly
disentangled what seemed to have become a
Gordian knot.

He was not only a brilliant scholar, but an
eloquent orator, and as such was chosen for
another important task, that of Professor in
Ecclesiastical Diplomacy and International Law
at the Academy of Noble Ecclesiastics, the papal
diplomatic training school. Even more onerous
was a further collaboration to which Gasparri, his
untiring mentor, chose him, that of Secretary
of the Commission for the Codification of Canon
Law. This was a monumental task, but with the
doggedness of a mountaineer, Gasparri had set
his teeth in it, though he knew that it would take
him all his life, if God spared him. The Law of
the Church was spread over numerous edicts and

bulls. Gasparri went to work to collect and co-ordinate them with characteristic thoroughness. He began by founding his own printing works, so that he could supervise it properly. When he had finished collecting all the material, he had it sent out to each of the 1,200 Bishops of the Catholic Community over the world, with instructions that every Bishop was to consult with three local lawyers, all sworn to secrecy. Thus some five thousand people collaborated in the codification.

Gasparri used to absent himself from the Vatican one day a week, the only break, but a regular one, in his iron routine of incessant work. Then he galloped round the countryside, inspected with the eye of an expert a little property he had outside the city gates, which his brother ran for him, and was farmer again, showing a new hand how to drive a plough. To thin and pale Pacelli he counselled a good daily walk : " We talk so much of heaven that a bit of earth underneath our feet will do us good." Pacelli obeyed. Even on the day before his election as Pope, he could be seen taking his stroll on the Pincio Hill overlooking Rome. His favourite recreation, however, was music, his violin ; he had the sense of melody born with

33

him, hence the melodious music of his eloquence. On Sundays he went to private Chamber Music Concerts in patrician houses, where he was a welcome guest ; very tall, very pale, his dreaming dark eyes underneath thick black curls, made him an apparition which one did not soon forget.

London got to know him as early as 1901 when he was the bearer of a handwritten letter of condolence from Pope Leo XIII to King Edward VII, on the death of Queen Victoria. Seven years later, a *Monsignore* then, he stayed with the Duke of Norfolk at St. James's Square during the London Eucharistic Congress. He must be the only Pope with a British decoration—once Pope they accept none—for in 1911 he attended the coronation of King George V in the suite of the Papal Envoy, Archbishop Granito Pignatelli di Belmonte. But his preference continued to go out to a simple curate's work ; he heard confessions in the little church where he served Mass in his youth, gave Sunday School lessons and preached occasionally, fine orations, over the preparation of which he took infinite pains.

V

NUNCIO MEETS KAISER

POPE PIUS X, not a brilliant mind, but a saintly pastor of souls, died from a broken heart shortly after the outbreak of the world war, in August, 1914. His successor was Benedict XV, who as Cardinal della Chiesa had been both Gasparri's and Pacelli's immediate superior. He nominated Cardinal Gasparri his Secretary-of-State, Monsignor Pacelli became head of the Congregation for Extraordinary Ecclesiastical Affairs.

In the Papal Archives there is a row of sixty heavy bundles of papers, dryly listed in impeccable Latin *De Caritate Sanctae Sedis Erga Gallos:* 1792-1803—"About the Assistance of the Holy See to the French," those clerics, aristocrats and citizens who had fled the dungeons and the guillotine of the French Revolution. That greatest tradition of the Father of Christendom, Benedict XV was determined to uphold. In December, 1914, he put proposals before the French and German Governments to exchange those prisoners of war who were unfit for further military service. Thirty thousand were thus cleared through Swiss territory. Thereupon the Pope suggested the return of civilians too young or too old for active service, 3,000 Belgians and 20,000 French from the occupied areas were in consequence released by Germany, while 10,000 wounded soldiers of both camps, at his further initiative, were brought to Switzerland in December, 1915, to recuperate. Prominent prisoners were pardoned through his efforts, and the Bishops were instructed to collect news of missing persons and prisoners of war, so as to lessen the suspense of their relatives at home. All this work was concentrated under Monsignor Pacelli, who worked literally day and night, having created a special office for the purpose and trained a specially chosen staff.

But the Pope's aspirations went further. He was biding the opportune moment for an intervention on a much greater scale in the cause of peace. At the end of April, 1917, he placed Eugenio Pacelli on the most advanced post in his scheme, that of Papal Nuncio at Munich. Nominally accredited to the Catholic Kingdom

of Bavaria, then still the most independent State
within the framework of the German Empire, it
was really his direct link with the Imperial
Government at Berlin, where under the Protestant Hohenzollerns a nunciature had not been
feasible. To mark the importance of his post,
Pacelli was elevated to the Titular Archbishopric
of Sardes and consecrated by the Pope himself
in the Sistine Chapel—which twenty-two years
later would see him elected Pope. With what
intensity Benedict must have prayed as,
enthroned on the high altar underneath
Michelangelo's "Last Judgment," he laid his
hands on the collaborator he had chosen for the
most difficult charge at the most difficult time,
invoking the solemn episcopal consecration :
"Receive the Holy Ghost " . . .

That summer it looked to neutral onlookers
as if there was some sort of a balance between
the positions of the two great armed camps.
The Central Powers, it is true, seemed to hold
the whip hand, for had they not occupied all
Belgium, Northern France, large tracts of
Russia, all Rumania and Serbia? But in reality
they were exhausted after their many victories.
The Allies, on the other hand, had only just
begun to organize their overseas supply and, great

as was the havoc wrought by the submarines, the steady flow of fresh recruits could not be stopped. Thus, Pope Benedict calculated, there was an honourable chance for both parties, since the Centrals' present strategic position and the Allies' enormous future reserves balanced each other.

When Nuncio Pacelli reached Munich to take up his first diplomatic post, he was at once received, with full regal pomp, at the residence of the Bavarian Prince Regent, to hand over his letters of credence. But a few days afterwards we find him already in Berlin and reporting a "very good reception" from the Imperial Chancellor, von Bethmann-Hollweg. Behind the scenes his first meeting with the Kaiser was quietly arranged. It took place on July 29th, 1917, in the Imperial Headquarters at Kreuznach, that delightful Baden Spa. War was not allowed to be forgotten in the city of roses and nightingales. All officers of the Imperial Household were in field grey ; only the Kaiser, though it was ten o'clock in the morning, had donned his full-dress uniform of a Prussian Field-Marshal, to receive the Nuncio. He remained standing the whole time of the audience, holding his helmet under his left arm.

Monsignor Pacelli handed His Majesty a
letter written in the Pope's own hand, soliciting
the Kaiser's help in the promotion of peace.
Wilhelm II read it then and there, and remarked
that in the previous December he himself had
already broached a peace offer, but without
result. Nuncio Pacelli emphasized that it needed
more detailed propositions, but it soon became
clear to the diplomat that the Kaiser did not
want another initiative, that he firmly believed in
the final victory of his troops. The Kaiser,
furthermore, had very fixed ideas of how the
Pope should conduct his affairs. He should
mobilise the Catholic Episcopate all over the
world in a moral peace offensive, and begin by
using his especial influence on Catholic States
by promoting peace between Italy and Austria.
When the Nuncio drew the Kaiser's attention
to the impractibility of such a scheme, since
there existed a strong war party in Italy against
Austria (led, amongst others, by the Editor of
the "Popolo d'Italia," a certain Benito
Mussolini) the Kaiser assured the Nuncio that
His Holiness "need not fear the scum." Warm-
ing up to his pet subject, strategy, he began to
outline how the Pope could defend the Vatican.
"I have been there myself," he told Pacelli, and

his easy fantasy quickly turned the palaces of the Vatican into a veritable fortress.

The Nuncio was more than amazed, he must have thought himself in a theatre instead of with the responsible head of the principal Central Power. Leaving the Kaiser's fancy to roam uninterruptedly over the defence of the Vatican, he patiently waited for the end of the Imperial theories, then deftly turning to practical use the Kaiser's obvious satisfaction with his own elocution, he elicited a promise to check the excessive German deportation of Belgian civilians. The Kaiser invited his distinguished guest to stay for lunch and had him placed at his right hand. Years later, in his *Gedanken und Erinnerungen* (" Musings and Recollections ") Wilhelm II gave this description of Nunçio Pacelli : " He has a distinguished sympathetic appearance, he is of a high intelligence and has impeccable manners ; in short, the prototype of a Prince of the Church." The Imperial description holds good to this day.

VI

AMBASSADOR OF PEACE

THE Papal Embassy, or Nunciature as it is called, was housed in Munich in a large gloomy-looking house in the centre of the diplomatic quarter of the Bavarian capital, the Brienner Strasse. It was austerely furnished, and even the bright crimson plush, the essence of distinction in those days, did not mitigate that austerity. This house was the frontal post in the peace campaign which Pope Benedict XV, after minute preparations, was to launch from the Vatican.

On June 13th, 1917, Cardinal-Secretary of State, Gasparri, had enquired from the Reich Government what its peace conditions were. A fortnight later Pacelli went again to Berlin and saw the Chancellor, who told him that Germany was prepared to restore Belgium and agree to an all-round limitation of armaments. But von Bethmann-Hollweg, who had at the outbreak of the war openly regretted the " sad necessity " of the violation of Belgium, fell from power a fortnight later. The Reichstag, however, in its resolution of July 19th, pronounced itself in favour of a peace without annexation. The British Premier, Lloyd George, in his speech in Glasgow, that same month, stressed Britain's readiness for a conciliatory peace on condition of a preliminary acceptance of the restoration of Belgium.

Never in any previous attempt had the two points of view come so near. The Pope now decided to concentrate all his efforts, and he instructed Pacelli to try and win the German Government for the Peace Points which he had drafted, and to which those President Wilson was to formulate more than a year later bear a marked resemblance: restoration of Belgium; return of the German Colonies; limitation of armament; freedom of the seas; and an International Court of Arbitration. Two days after Pacelli's call on the Berlin Foreign Office he was informed that these proposals seemed to form an acceptable basis and would now be put before the Kaiser who was at Vienna.

In London the heads of the Allied States were to come together for an important inter-allied conference on August 7th. That was an opportunity Cardinal Gasparri did not want to miss.

He urged Pacelli to convince Berlin that there was no time to lose. Monsignor Pacelli, on wiring Berlin, was requested to stay in Munich as the Berlin Foreign Office was convinced that an agreement on the Papal Points would be reached within a week.

Kept waiting and waiting, fearing the worst, Pope Benedict XV decided to force the issue. On August 14th the Papal Envoys in all capitals handed His Holiness' Peace Note to the Monarchs and Presidents of the world. A supreme effort to save Europe from committing suicide, it proclaimed instead of might, "the moral of right." It was eloquent in sentiment, and in its practicability it went even further than the League of Nations which was to be born some years later, for in proposing an International Court, it pleaded for power against those who would not want to submit. In fact, it advanced suggestions with which, twenty years later, statesmen like Mr. Winston Churchill and Lord Davies tried to rescue the Geneva institution from its utter inertia. The Papal Note further pleaded for an all-round renunciation of damages and a limitation of armaments; this, the practical Pope argued, would in its relief of the national budgets soon make good each

43

nation's war losses. Instead, the preposterous penalty imposed on the vanquished at Versailles not only came to nought, but wrecked sound economic life and international trade for generations, bringing static unemployment in its wake.

The Pope's plan was a grand plan—and a most sensible one. Had it been accepted, the peoples of Europe would have been spared much of the agony which they have gone through since. There were, of course, serious drawbacks. France felt that this plan might cost her the rewinning of Alsace-Lorraine on which she had set her mind since 1871, and that, too, at a moment when the French trenches were being reinforced by increasing contingents of fresh American troops. England, through her Minister to the Holy See, Count de Salis, explained to Cardinal Gasparri that an unequivocal German declaration that she would restore Belgium and indemnify her for the terrible losses inflicted upon an innocent people, was the *conditio sine qua non* of any proposal which the British Government was prepared to entertain.

There were petty objections, however, which doomed the Papal peace action which had galvanized millions of tortured minds and bodies back into hope. In the Treaty of London, by

44

which the Allied Powers had roped in Italy,
formerly the Confederate of Germany and
Austria, a secret clause had been inserted at
the insistence of the then professedly anti-
clerical Government of Italy, promising them
that the Allied Powers would not admit any
Papal conciliation. Times indeed have changed
since !

But worse was a similar objection working on
the German side. There, von Bethmann-
Hollweg had been succeeded as Chancellor by
Dr. Michaelis, a pedantic Prussian official and a
sectarian fanatic who hated to see a Papal effort
succeed. In vain Nuncio Pacelli pleaded with
him, that " If a clear and unequivocal assurance
can be given on Belgium, the crucial point,
a peace honourable to all is assured and Your
Excellency's name will be immortal." A
courteous note followed which, in modern
parlance, instead of slamming any doors left
them all open. Cardinal Gasparri scanned it and
summed it up in one of those characteristic words
of his : " Worthless ! " For Belgium was not
mentioned at all. Indefatigable, Pacelli again
set to work, and finally Dr. Michaelis' real reply
came It mentioned Belgium's restoration, but
in a prudent legal phrasing, so hemmed in by

D

' buts,' ' ifs ' and ' howevers,' that it could not be turned to any useful account.

To-day it makes sorry reading, this game of bluff and of intermittent delays, played by the diplomats whilst the youth of Europe was bleeding to death in the mud of Flanders, on the plains of Russia, on Balkan mountain ranges and along Italian river valleys. One golden thread runs through it all : the tenacity of purpose, the purity of aim of Nuncio Pacelli who did everything humanly possible to smooth the way to a compromise. To-day the effort seems almost forgotten, it never secured the Nobel Prize—but never has a nobler attempt been made in the cause of peace. That evening when the last German note was received, a German friend came to see the Nuncio. They sat long after dusk in the silent unlit study at the Brienner Strasse. Pacelli could hardly control his deep emotion. " Everything is lost," he sighed, then, visionary, " your poor country, too." . . .

Henceforward he occupied himself chiefly with the organization of relief of human distress, so rampant in Central Europe, from the starving children in the blockaded Reich to the caged-up Allied prisoners of war over whose well-being he watched incessantly.

VII

UNDER COMMUNIST THREATS

PEACE, which had been honourably possible in 1917 through the Papal intermediary, came to Germany fifteen months later, under utter surrender. A starved and completely misguided people, seeing its greatest virtue, that of faithful discipline, grossly betrayed by its leaders, fell into convulsions of revolution. Nowhere in Germany did revolution rear its head in more ugly guise than in the Bavarian capital. The Red Flag of the Spartakus movement flew from the royal residence. The Government, the Diplomatic Corps, the Inter-Allied Relief Commission, all had fled to Bamberg in Northern Bavaria. For the Russians of the neighbouring prison camps who had been hailed as Bolshevist brothers, armed and placed to guard the barricades in the streets of the capital, recognized no authority whatsoever.

Monsignor Pacelli was the only one who

stayed in Munich. From the meagre provisions
of the Nunciature he brought food to the children
in the poorest quarters. When later Munich was
relieved, all that was left in the Papal Embassy
was some stale bread and cocoa. So undaunted
was the Nuncio that he went out on these errands
of mercy every day in his black limousine until
the Reds commandeered it. A band of seven
armed brigands one day actually invaded his
home. Calmly the tall, forty-three years old
dignitary met them and enquired their business.
Whether it was the cool contempt of the piercing
dark eyes and of the thin lips in his earnest white
face—whether it was the high dignity which he
represented with such unflinching courage, or
the total lack of any physical fear—the Reds,
having demanded " money and treasures " and
been met with a curt refusal, contented themselves with taking his car away. Day after day
the Nuncio telephoned to the Town Hall to whatever chieftain was in power, pointing out that as
representative of a foreign sovereign his
possessions were inviolable by International Law.
The officials became so annoyed that one of
them threatened " to come and shoot the whole
nest." " *Bitte schön* "—You are welcome—

said the Nuncio coolly, putting down the receiver.

That day thirteen aristocrats had been shot in cold blood. The Italian Military Attaché, who had stayed in Munich to guard the Italian Legation building, had warned Pacelli that there was a plan afoot to take the Nunciature with machine guns. But all that happened was that Pacelli got his car back in the end. Many years before, the young altar boy had confided to his mother that he would like to become a missionary. Now, a Nuncio with the titular rank of Archbishop, there was no flinching from his duty to stay at his post and thus impart confidence to the stricken population. These were his missionary days.

After General von Epp had delivered the capital, Pacelli was its most popular diplomat. The only time he left Munich in the ensuing years, apart from his annual holiday, was when he went on his special mission to report on the situation in the Ruhr district. The French had occupied this industrial nerve centre of Germany—and that with black troops—to ".punish" the default on the impossible Reparation payments. Pacelli flew to the danger zone, and after a personal survey sent an exhaustive report to the Vatican. This formed

the basis for the Pope's letter to his Secretary-
of-State, in which His Holiness massed the
moral force of the Church against this Ruhr
adventure. It was, by the way, France's action
in the Ruhr which, in its unnecessary and
provoking indignities, years after the signing of
Peace, did more than anything else to fan the
tiny flame of revenge which the unknown Adolf
Hitler had lit in Munich about that time with his
seven-men-strong Nazi Party. The Papal Letter
meant to be, at the same time, an approval of
the plan of Mr. Charles Evans Hughes, to-day
President of the Supreme Court of the U.S.A.,
then Secretary of State of President Coolidge,
to have a tribunal of impartial experts decide
upon the capacity of Germany to pay reparations.

In 1925, his work in Munich crowned with a
Concordat between the Holy See and Bavaria,
Eugenio Pacelli was promoted as Nuncio to
Berlin, accredited to the Reich Government.
By unwritten usage—a right acknowledged in
every capital of the world with the exception of
London and Washington—he became, as Papal
Ambassador, Dean of the Diplomatic Corps.
He had presented his credentials to the stocky,
former saddle-maker, socialist President Fritz
Ebert, and so firm were their personal bonds—

though Ebert was a born Catholic who no longer practised the religion of his youth—that after Ebert's death Pacelli was often a guest at the table of his widow. Ebert's successor as President, Field-Marshal von Hindenburg, a staunch and strict Protestant, took such a liking to the Roman prelate that he once showed him the prayer his father had written for his confirmation. Viscount d'Abernon, the first British Ambassador in post-war Berlin, has called Pacelli in his Memoirs the best informed man in Berlin. He was to be seen in the salon of Dr. Stresemann, the dynamic Foreign Minister, and to be heard at popular meetings in the enormous *Sport Palast*, Berlin's Albert Hall.

Four years he worked patiently at the Concordat between Prussia and the Holy See. He won his victories by sheer patience, making use of every opportunity, never giving up, never letting himself be swayed by outside influences. He was superior to all in the subtle art of diplomacy. When the term " Concordat " caused excitement among Protestant die-hards, he named it a " solemn convention." What is in a word ! The German Protestant Press Service in a tribute on his departure lauded his ten years' work in Germany as that of " a sower amidst ruins." It sums him up admirably.

On being nominated a Cardinal in December, 1929, and called to the supreme council of the Church in Rome, he had to relinquish his post in Berlin. President von Hindenburg was deeply moved at the farewell audience. " Germany," he said, " will never forget your share in the pacification of our country." The Nuncio was driven in an open carriage to the Anhalter Station, accompanied by Dr. Klausener, then the President of the Berlin Catholic Action (murdered in his Ministry during the July massacre of 1934). Deputations of all organisations, from student clubs to trade unions, holding torches, lined the route through Berlin's busiest streets, *Hoching* and *Heiling* the Papal Envoy at his triumphant leave-taking. On the carpeted and flower-bedecked station platform the Cabinet and the Diplomatic Corps had foregathered to bid him farewell in person. But hardly had the express left the suburbs of Berlin behind it, roaring through the woods of the Brandenburg Mark in the darkness of the night, when in the saloon carriage of Monsignor Pacelli the portable was unlocked and the Nuncio settled down to type his letters.

VIII

SECRETARY OF STATE

THE recall of Nuncio Pacelli to Rome, his nomination as member of that small body of the Pope's intimate advisers, the Cardinals of the Roman Curia, heralded great changes in the high ranks of the Vatican.

The Secretary of State, Cardinal Gasparri, was approaching his eighties in a zenith of administrative success and in unbounded health. He had been the main mover in the conciliation between Italy and the Holy See, he had seen his monumental work for the codification of Canon Law crowned by the issuing of the new Codex. He desired to retire whilst his health still allowed him a quiet aftermath of a well spent life. Already decorated with the Collar of the Annunziata Order, which made him a cousin of the King, like Mussolini, he was presented by the Pope with a small *palazzo* in the shadow of the Capitol, the State promptly paying him the honour of posting a guard of honour in front of it.

The choice of a successor presented no difficulty to the Pontiff, who had had his eye on Pacelli for a long time. He knew of his early training in the Vatican State Department under the incomparable Gasparri. In fact, when Prefect of the Vatican Library, Monsignor Achille Ratti had been consulted frequently by Monsignor Pacelli, then at work on the Codification of Canon Law A sympathy had sprung up which ripened when, on his way back as Apostolic Visitator in Poland, after the Peace of Brest-Litowsk, Monsignor Ratti returned to Rome by way of Munich. He stayed at the Nunciature and they had a long exchange of views—this time not on books and jurisprudence but on political affairs. Neither of them could have foreseen that evening in the Brienner Strasse that they were destined to work together intimately for long years, one as Head of the Church, the other as Secretary of State, and that the younger was to succeed the older.

Shortly afterwards Monsignor Ratti himself had become Nuncio, at Warsaw, under circumstances of the most trying character. The Bolshevik army stood before the gates of the Polish capital. In a conference at his house of the diplomatic corps, in which Herbert

Hoover, later President of the United States, then American Relief Commissioner, participated, it was decided that the foreign dignitaries should leave Warsaw. Only Nuncio Ratti refused ; he stayed at his post, and after General Weygand's strategy had averted the danger, the Polish Parliament passed a motion of homage to the Papal Nuncio for his courageous action which had done so much to avert panic and to strengthen the confidence of the population. Small wonder that, when Nuncio Ratti became Pope, he remembered with especial satisfaction the parallel action of his then colleague, the Nuncio at Munich, who had stayed at his post right through the Red terror. That was the sort of fibre of which he himself was made. Hence he had followed closely the political career of his most successful and most popular Nuncio.

Even closer was the Pontiff's connection with another member of the Pacelli family, the Nuncio's brother. Francesco Pacelli, like his father, was a Vatican lawyer. The Pope had chosen him as his trusted go-between in the difficult negotiations with Mussolini to achieve the conciliation between Vatican and Quirinal Rome, between the Church and the State. Over a period of some years there were more than a hundred secret interviews between Francesco Pacelli and Mussolini. Every interview had been carefully prepared by the Pope; equally carefully he studied the outcome of every single encounter and prepared the next step. There is not a word, not a comma, in the Lateran Treaty which Pacelli, the advocate, had not discussed minutely with the Pope, the Duce, and Gasparri. The outcome was a triumph. The Pope had given all he could—the territory which he reserved was not much larger than a good-sized golf course; the financial indemnity by Italy, huge though it seems, was but a fraction of the property and treasures which the Pope had lost in 1870. When the Treaty was signed in the Lateran Palace—restoring to the Pontiff the sovereign rights of a Temporal Ruler which he had never ceased to claim since his States, the provinces of Central Italy, were taken from him in 1870, and for which he had voluntarily proclaimed himself the Prisoner of the Vatican—Francesco Pacelli stood behind Mussolini and Gasparri as they signed. He had been created a hereditary Marquis that morning as a special mark of Papal favour.

On February 10th, 1930, Cardinal Pacelli was nominated Papal Secretary of State, a high office he was destined to fill for nine years, unique preparation for the highest dignity in the world.

Let us look at Eugenio Pacelli as he was then. But for his much-greyed hair, he is the same man to-day. He is tall, majestically so, for his height is emphasized by stately ecclesiastical garb, the flowing black cassock with the vivid touch of its crimson silk seams and long row of crimson buttons. Above the broad crimson sash hangs the dazzling pectoral cross on a heavy gold chain. A little crimson skull cap covers the tonsure in his thick and curly hair. One is impressed by his stature—truly royal when he wears the ermine cape and the trailing silk robes of ceremonial dress—but one is completely fascinated by his countenance. His face is a perfect oval, of olive complexion, with the lofty brow of the scholar, and deep-set, jet-black eyes behind gold-rimmed spectacles. Of great distinction, his suavity puts every visitor completely at ease, but even with the highest of them he preserves the aloofness of his high calling. He talks with great courtesy and consideration, but his gentle eyes probe beyond the core of things, though one is never aware of being rapidly sized-up.

Entering the Basilica of St. Peter amidst heralding trumpets for a great ceremony, robed

57

in gorgeous vestments, he is every inch a Prelate,
but when saying Mass he becomes transformed
into a simple priest, and his face lights up with
the moving devotion of one profoundly aware of
his own unworthiness as the intermediary at the
Altar between God and men. Once, when his
long shining Packard was held up by the fair
in a mountain village on an Italian summer
morning, he sat rigidly in the cushions, reading
his breviary, and nothing of the pandemonium
round him diverted his attention for a second.
Seated on a silk-covered settee in front of the
enormous window in the high, light and cool
study of the Secretary of State in the Vatican
Palace, looking out on the Damascus courtyard,
he talks to his visitors with an earnestness and
intensity which most of the highest-placed of this
world keep only for their equals. One feels the
probing of his earnest, deep eyes, one is again
aware of the utter serenity—for it is far more
than mere acquired discipline—of a man at peace
with himself, and one senses the spirituality of
this high dignitary who has always remained by
vocation the curate of souls.

The few anecdotes that are known about him
typify the man. There is his barber who used to
come occasionally to the Vatican to cut his hair,

and who was amazed at the Cardinal shaving himself without soap, with an electric razor. He would not believe it until the Cardinal asked him to rub his cheek. There is the five-year-old son of the then French Ambassador in Berlin, d'Ormesson, who, when Nuncio Pacelli came to say good-bye to the family, muttered an " *Au revoir, mon vieux,*" which, so everyone hoped fervently, the Nuncio would not have heard. Years later the newly-elected Pope, receiving the homage of the Marquis d'Ormesson, asked him, with a twinkle in his eye : " Tell me, does your little son still call visitors ' *mon vieux* '? "

Few know of his reluctance in accepting the Cardinalate. His friend, Cardinal von Faulhaber, the great Archbishop of Munich, had told him about a convent in Switzerland, " Stella Maris," on the Rorschacherberg. There, between the mountains, the lake, and the forests, he went ever since 1917 regularly for his annual holiday, delighting in long walks, so that the children began to know him and hailed him in their local dialect with a sunny " Greeting, Father." He became so popular among them that they used to flock to him for confession, which he loved to take on Saturday evenings to relieve the " other " curates of the local parish church. On

a walk during one of these Swiss holidays a
telegram was delivered to him. "*Fervida-
mente,*" it said cryptically—"Heartiest con-
gratulations." "Do you understand that?"
asked the Nuncio, handing the telegram to his
walking companion. When the latter suggested
that the Cardinalate, about which rumours had
already begun to appear in the press, must have
materialized, Pacelli was so amazed that he
lapsed into his native tongue. "*Non posso
capire*"—"I cannot understand it, I have
begged the Pope so insistently to put me in
charge of a diocese." That same evening he
left for Rome to try and change the Pope's mind.
It was of no avail.

What precisely is the Secretary of State? He
is, so to speak, the Pope's Prime Minister-cum-
Foreign Secretary. There is in the Vatican
Archives a letter in which Sixtus V enumerates
the qualities which a Secretary of State needs.
"He must know everything, have read everything, understand everything, but he must say
nothing."

Pacelli, indeed, has an encyclopædic knowledge. He speaks eight languages fluently.
Generally those phenomena who are supposed to
speak many languages have a vocabulary as

(D 1132)

limited as that of a hotel porter. But Cardinal Pacelli, addressing an International Press Conference in Rome, spoke for more than an hour in seven languages : Italian, French, English, German, Portuguese, Spanish, and finally in Latin. All without a written note before him, without any ,hesitancy, without any slowing-up of speech or searching for words, swinging easily from one language into the other, his soft voice vibrant with the intensity of what he desired to impart to this select international audience. Of course, he has always been a magnificent preacher ; as an orator his secret is that he says the truth with force, but also with grace. He gives every sermon the careful preparation of an artist, but he remains natural, disdains pathos. His speeches are built up with the logic on which true Romans pride themselves. He electrifies the masses by his personality, the dignity of his noble appearance and his eloquent and fascinating gesticulations. His appeals go from heart to heart, the listener senses the preacher's own burning conviction.

He spoke with equal eloquence in the Berlin Sportpalast, in the Cathedral of Lisieux, and before the Parliament of Rio de Janeiro. His German *" Gesammelte Reden "* are as magni-

E

ficent as is the " *Triptique* " of the sermons
which he delivered in France. To master
another language is to double one's culture and
wisdom, it has been said, and with truth. By
that reckoning Pope Pius XII must be the
wisest and most cultured man living.

IX

TRIUMPHS AND SORROWS

His high burdens, once taken up, increased as his fame spread. A month after his appointment as Secretary of State came his nomination as Archpriest of St. Peter's, virtually that of Dean of the greatest Cathedral in the world. Later he became also Camerlengo, which brings with it the temporary headship of the Church during a vacancy of the Papal Throne.

Paramount remained the all-important office of Secretary of State. They were eventful years devoted to widely varying tasks. His searching mind was set to work first of all on an agreement interpreting certain regulations of the Italian Concordat with the Holy See, which had followed the Lateran Treaty, solving some of the minor and restricting some of the latent misunderstandings inherent in the Church's relations with an absolute State not sure yet of its own ideology. When later the Fascist regime demanded the disbandment of Catholic Action,

the Pope issued an Encyclical on the matter.
Realising that through a censorship of press-
telegrams and other " delays " Mussolini might
use a chance of checkmating the Encyclical
before it could reach the public, Pacelli entrusted
a young American Monsignor working at the
State Department, Francis Spellman, now Archbishop of New York, to fly an advance copy from
the Vatican to Paris, to release it there to the
news agencies and press correspondents. Thus
it burst upon the Fascist Government as a total
surprise. Later, of course, the Vatican's own
radio transmission station—designed by no less
an expert than the Marquis Marconi, President
of the Papal Academy of Science—made such
devices unnecessary.

Pacelli set to work to conclude further
concordats—amongst others, one with Austria—
and although that with Yugo-Slavia failed to be
put in operation at the eleventh hour, after a
stormy ratification in the Belgrade Chamber,
Pacelli's policy vastly improved the status of the
Catholic Church in that country as it notably did
in all the Slav countries of Central and South-
Eastern Europe.

There were triumphs, such as the return to
the fold of official France. The Church's

" eldest daughter " had long been estranged from the paternal house. But with a Papal diplomacy which actively supported a positive international peace policy, common ground was soon reached. Relations grew stronger and more cordial. At the end of the Holy Year, 1935, commemorating the Nineteenth Centenary of the Redemption, the Pope sent Pacelli to represent him as his special Legate at a solemn Triduum at the Grotto of Lourdes. But even more important politically was Cardinal Pacelli's mission to Lisieux, in the summer of 1937, to consecrate the Basilica of Saint Thérèse, that young Carmelite nun who died at the age of twenty-four to become the Mediator of modern needs. France received him with royal honours, the Prime Minister and the members of his Popular Front Cabinet were at the Gare de Lyon in Paris to await him, the Republican Guard presented arms and played the Papal Hymn. But for his weak old age, so it was announced, the Pope would have come himself ; now he had appointed "his closest collaborator," whose sermons both in Lisieux and under the hallowed roof of the Paris church of Our Lady of Victories were of pentecostal eloquence.

Under the Red dictatorships of Mexico and

Russia the Church had been vilely persecuted, and conditions in Germany were almost as sorrowful as in Spain, split by a bloody civil war. The Abyssinian conquest had been a most painful time for the Father of Christendom. Pacelli could not condemn the adventure outright, just as no Papal condemnation had been possible against England's rape of the Boer Republics in South Africa, at the outset of this century of violence. But the Vatican took great pains to make it clear that whatever any Italian prelate did or said, was done or said as an Italian citizen and not as a spokesman for the Vatican. A neat distinction, and the only one possible, where justice and humanity clash with patriotism as so many zealots see it. After all, the Church is not there to look after the ever-changing pattern of power politics, but after eternal verities. When Faith was assailed, the Vatican rose with all its might and power to defend its very foundations.

That defence was brilliantly exemplified in the historic Encyclical, *Mit brennender Sorge* ("With Deep Anxiety"). It was, of course, composed by the aged Pope himself, but many are the passages which resound with the advice, in fact betray the pen of his closest collaborator, to-day his successor.

66

Cardinal Pacelli had always been known for his strong German leanings. The simplicity, energy and reliability which were once the best characteristics of the German people, conformed to his own. Hitler changed all that, although one of his first acts was to send von Papen to Rome to negotiate a new Concordat with Cardinal Pacelli, who guaranteed to curb the political activity of the Catholic clergy in Germany. In return Vice-Chancellor von Papen promised in Hitler's name that there would be no discrimination against the leaders of the recently dissolved Centre Party of Germany, and that the Church would enjoy all its rights in complete freedom. For a few months the agreement was grudgingly observed; soon encroachments began once more and grew stronger and louder. When at the Silver Sacerdotal Jubilee of the Cardinal-Archbishop of Cologne, Dr. Schulte, Cardinal Pacelli sent him a message of congratulation, praising him for combating neo-pagan ideas, Nazi retaliations came promptly in the form of a disgusting campaign against monks and nuns for violating the currency laws and good morals. No defence, no counter-action, was allowed.

Cardinal Pacelli saw clearly from the outset

how there was more at stake than the attack on
the Church, that the whole structure of international relationship was in the balance. He saw
in what was happening the grim shadow of the
future, and he surveyed the changing political
scene with growing concern. "No one can
fathom what Pacelli means to us," the Pope
once said to Cardinal von Faulhaber, the
courageous Archbishop of Munich.

The Encyclical opens with the declaration
that the Concordat which Pacelli had negotiated
was moved "by a sincere desire to render an
essential service to the peaceful development and
welfare of the German people," and then the
Pope, in unequivocal language, castigates the
Nazi policy of broken pledges.

" If the tree of peace planted by Us with pure
intention in German soil has not borne the fruit
We desired in the interests of your people," says
the Encyclical, " no one in the whole world who
has eyes to see or ears to hear can say to-day
that the fault lies with the Church and with her
Supreme Head. The experience of the past
years fixes the responsibility. It discloses
intrigues which from the beginning had no other
aim than a war of extermination. In the furrows
in which We had laboured to sow the seeds of

true peace, others sowed the tares of suspicion, discord, hatred, calumny, of secret and open fundamental hostility to Christ and His Church, fed from a thousand different sources and making use of every available means. On them and on them alone and on their silent and vocal protectors rests the responsibility that now on the horizon of Germany there is to be seen not the rainbow of peace but the threatening storm-clouds of destructive religious wars.''

''Venerable Brethren,'' thus the Pope continues his address to the German Episcopate, '' We have not grown weary of presenting to the rulers who guide the destinies of your nation the inevitable consequences of tolerating or worse still of favouring such tendencies. We have done all We could to defend the sanctity of the solemn pledges, the inviolability of obligations freely entered into, against theories and practices which, if officially approved, must destroy all confidence and render intrinsically worthless every future pledge. When the time comes to place before the eyes of the world these endeavours of Ours, all right-minded persons will know where to look for the peace-makers and where to look for the peace-breakers. Anyone who has any sense of truth left in his mind and even a shadow of the feeling of justice left in his heart will have to admit that, in the difficult and eventful years which followed the Concordat, every word and every action of Ours was ruled by loyalty to the terms of the agreement ; but also he will have to recognize with surprise and deep disgust that the unwritten law of the other party has been arbitrary misinterpretation of agreements, evasion of agreements, evasion of the meaning of agreements, and finally more or less open violation of agreements.''

Seldom can a gloved hand have hit harder ! And in expounding the fundamental precepts of Catholic religion, in fact those of all Christianity, the Pope does not hesitate to say : '' Whoever transposes Race or People, the State or Constitution, the executive or other fundamental elements of human society (which in the natural order have an essential and honourable place), from the scale of earthly values and makes them the ultimate norm of all things, even of religious values, and deifies them with the idolatrous cult, perverts and falsifies the divinely created and appointed order of things ''—or to lash, in another place : '' the arbitrary revelations that certain contemporary prophets try to extract from the so-called myth of blood and race.''

Then, laying his finger on the outrageous statement, that "right is what is advantageous to the German people," the Pope hits out :

"This fundamental principle, cut off from moral law, would mean in relations between states a perpetual state of war amongst the various nations ; in the life of the state it confuses advantage and right, and refuses to recognize the fundamental fact that man as a person possesses rights given him by God which must be preserved from every attempt by the community to deny, suppress, or hinder their exercise. Whoever transgresses this order shakes the pillars of society and imperils its tranquillity, security, and even its existence."

Over the length and breadth of the German land this Papal admonition was read out on Easter Sunday, 1937, from the pulpit of every Catholic Church. It is destined to remain a great human document for all time.

Here attention may well be drawn to Pacelli's advice and assistance with the other famous Encyclicals of his predecessor—those on Christian Marriage (*Casti Connubii*) ; on the Social Order (*Quadragesimo Anno*) ; on the Apostolate of the Laity (*Non Abbiamo Bisogno*) ; on Unemployment and the Economic

Crisis (*Nova Impendet*), and that moving
pastoral letter, named like all Encyclicals after
its opening words, *Caritate Christi Compulsi*,
" The Love of Christ Compels Us." This Encyclical deals with the needs and troubles of our
time, tracing them to an accumulation of the
wealth of nations in the hands of a small group
of individuals and to that exorbitant nationalism,
which the Pope ranked, together with communism, as the revolt of men against God.

The duties of the Papacy demand spiritual
even more than worldly wisdom. The Church
does not aspire to temporal power. Its foreign
policy has only one aim : the welfare of the
Catholic community in every country, no matter
what form of Government it enjoys, whether it
is democracy or dictatorship, provided its effects
are just and charitable. Wherever that spiritual
well-being is endangered through laws or
measures restricting the primary right of the
individual to call his soul his own and to serve
God according to the dictates of his own conscience, the Church stands up against such a
violation of the fundamental principle of
Catholicity. In doing so it serves the cause of
all Christendom, of which it is the spearhead.

X

MEETING THE NEW WORLD

ONE of Cardinal Pacelli's most spectacular journeys was that to South America in the autumn of 1934. Officially delegated as Papal Legate to the Eucharistic Congress at Buenos Aires, he was fêted by the Argentines with all the splendour due to the historic innovation of a Papal Secretary of State's first official mission abroad. The President of the Republic and the whole Government bid him welcome. In a Spanish of pure Castilian accent he spoke to an audience of one and a half million people gathered at the closing demonstration in Palermo Park, on " Peace Between Men." As he left Buenos Aires the sirens of ships and the whistles of factories gave him a tumultuous farewell. Even greater, if possible, was his welcome at Rio de Janeiro, where he addressed the Brazilian Deputies assembled in Parliament and the Supreme Court in session, in faultless Portuguese.

Two years later, he used his annual holiday to pay a visit to the United States. With the revenue cutter in New York harbour, batteries of film and press cameras boarded the Italian liner "Conte di Savoia." One of the enterprising Yankee photographers, perched on a lifeboat for greater advantage, shouted excitedly : "Hey, Mr. Pope, look this way ! " He was, indeed, the highest visitor, barring ruling royalty, whom the New World had ever welcomed. The Cardinal Secretary of State posed with charming willingness and, when the interviewing was about to start, handed to the pressmen a typewritten document which told of his happiness to be in the United States, "the territory of a great people who know how to unite so beautifully and nobly a sense of discipline with the exercise of a just, legitimate, and well-ordered liberty." "Here, gentlemen, is my entrance ticket to your country," was his disarming excuse, and not another statement was to be got of him.

A cordon of city police, hands linked, had to provide him a way through the kneeling multitude on Brooklyn Pier, where he mounted his car to convey him to the Long Island home which the Duchess Brady, the late American-born million-

aire wife of the present Irish Minister to the
Vatican, had given to the Jesuit Order. Pacelli
enjoyed America like an American ; he drove
along the seventeen-miles-long Triborough
Bridge, halting the car three times to get out
and inspect the structure₁; he was whisked up to
the 102nd floor of the Empire State Building by
ex-Governor Al Smith ; he was officially received
by Mayor La Guardia at City Hall.

When it became known that he had made
several visits (special correspondents of all the
big newspaper chains had been assigned to him
and followed him wherever he went) as to the
new headquarters of the Knights of Columbus
at New Haven, Conn., proceeding from there to
New England and addressing seven hundred
priests at Boston, Mass., telegrams and letters
from all over the American continent began to
pour in upon him with pressing invitations.

He fulfilled first his original plans to visit
Philadelphia and Washington. In his speech to
the University there—spoken with a correctness
of English unfamiliar to American audiences—at
his promotion as Doctor *honoris causa*, he
revealed that, early in this century, he had been
invited by that University to become its Professor
of Roman Law, but that the Pope had desired

him to remain in Rome. His oration was devoted
to "Religion and Science," the harmony
existing between faith and science, between the
supernatural and the natural.

He visited the Capitol and was the guest of
honour at the luncheon of the National Press
Club, the organization of Washington Correspondents. Here he made an impassioned plea to
his four hundred journalist hosts to pool the
whole of their enormous influence for peace.
From the Press Club he was whirled at high
speed, with siren-screaming motorcycle out-
riders and accompanying police squad cars to
Mount Vernon. He did more than lay a wreath
on the grave of George Washington, he stood a
moment in silent prayer on the hallowed resting-
place of the first President of America.

The enormous success of his trip and the
world-wide attention which it attracted made the
Cardinal decide to cover as much of the territory
of the States as his limited time-table would
allow. He chartered a Boeing passenger 'plane
from American Airlines and set out to meet
the rest of the United States, which with some
twenty-two millions of well-organized Catholics
is one of the bulwarks of the Church to-day.
Thus he went to Cleveland ; from there to Notre

(D 1132)

Dame University; he was kept flying for half an hour because of bad weather above Chicago aerodrome before he could land. ("No apologies"—thus the Cardinal waved the explanation of the aerodrome officials away. "Thank you for giving me a chance to catch up with my reading!") From Chicago to St. Paul; then over the great mountain divide to San Francisco, which gave him a tumultuous welcome, and where the civic authorities asked him to bless the gigantic Oakland Bridge, the latest world wonder. From Los Angeles over the Boulder Dam to Kansas City, with numerous stops; then Cincinnati, and, with a detour over Niagara Falls, back to New York.

Night travel, public receptions, appearances, speeches, inaugurations, banquets, laying of corner stones, receiving of degrees, conferences with the ecclesiastical dignitaries—nothing tired him out. He had a special table installed in front of his leather arm-chair in the aeroplane so that he could type his letters and prepare his speeches on his portable. On one of the last days of his stay he lunched with President Roosevelt at the latter's home in Hyde Park, New York State. When pressed for a comment, he escaped smilingly, "I enjoyed lunching with

F

a typical American family." But the pressman who described a scene at St. Patrick's Cathedral in New York when the slender, austere figure of this great dignitary knelt before the High Altar, touched the real chord : he had never seen anyone " pray like that."

Back in Rome, he found a dedicated portrait of the Pope as a homecoming gift. In four weeks he had travelled 30,000 miles. One may well accept the authenticity of Pacelli's remark when, immediately after his election to the Papacy, already dressed in his white silk cassock, he went to the Vatican sick room where Cardinal Marchetti, his friend from college days, lay ill. He sat down on the chair next to his bed ; then, his gaze travelling out of the window to the distant Alban mountains, faintly flushed by the last rays of the day, he suddenly said : " Now I shall not be able to travel any more . . ."

No one destined to become Pope has ever been so much in the public eye. To literally millions, in both hemispheres, he is a man they have come face to face with. In our days of close-ups, of news magazines, broadcasted commentaries and names that make news, a man occupying one of the highest international positions has no chance of keeping out of the limelight. Amongst all

78

pomp and splendour, however, Pacelli always remained at heart the priest. When last year he acted as Papal Legate to the Eucharistic Congress at Budapest, his special train arrived there at 10.20 in the morning ; a reception at the station followed ; then a state drive to the Royal Palace, where he was to stay, and where shortly after twelve he made use of the first quiet interval to say his Mass in the palace chapel. Which means that from midnight onwards through all the tiring ceremonies of the long morning he had fasted to be able to do so. It throws a light on his piety, just as does the sole personal bequest of Pope Pius XI, who in his testament gave Pacelli the chalice he had used for his own daily Mass.

CORONATION

WITH all the splendour and solemnity of Roman ritual, Eugenio Pacelli was crowned Pope on that early March Sunday of 1939.

The ceremony of the coronation, being the highest, is the most impressive and the longest of all functions of the Church. It took more than an hour alone for the procession, bringing the Pope from his state apartments in the Pontifical Palace, where he had been robed, to reach the High Altar in St. Peter's Basilica. It was preceded by Swiss Guards in their uniforms of yellow, blue and red, and with enormous halberds. Then came a Master of Ceremonies and other members of the Papal Household, Procurators of the Ecclesiastical Colleges, the Pope's preachers and confessors, and the heads of all the religious orders, monks and friars, many barefooted and with ropes for girdles. The apostolic messengers in violet soutanes, consistorial advocates, honorary chamberlains,

choristers of the Sistine Chapel, auditors of the
Rota in surplices and the Masters of the Sacred
Palaces, followed by two of the Pope's private
chaplains. They carried the mitre which he was
to wear during the Mass. An officer of the
Signatura carried the thurible for the incense.
An auditor of the Rota in white tunic carried the
Pope's cross, walking between seven officers
who bore seven candles. They were followed by
the Penitentiaries of St. Peter's in white
chasubles, mitred Abbots, Commanders of the
Order of the Holy Ghost, Oriental Bishops and
Archbishops in splendid vestments, Bishops and
Archbishops acting as attendants at the Papal
throne, Patriarchs, Cardinal Deacons, Cardinal
Priests, and Cardinal Bishops, with ermine capes
over their trailing crimson silk robes.

Then came the Pope in solemn majesty,
carried above the great concourse of people ; he
sat in the Chair of State in which he was borne
almost motionless, huge peacock-feathered fans
waving over his head. He was robed in a great
white cope, embroidered in gold over his vestments of white. On his head was a mitre adorned
with precious stones. His bearing was impressive.
His tall, frail frame, his collected countenance,
his wonderful eyes, his grace of gesture, his

perfect poise: a flawless picture. Rocking slightly from time to time, the chair was carried by grooms in renaissance liveries, crimson knee breeches and liveries of red damask. Near by were two privy chamberlains—their red capes trimmed with ermine, and candelabra in their hands.

When he reached the Chapel of the Blessed Sacrament, Pius XII left his chair for a moment of adoration, and was then carried to the nave of the Chapel of St. Gregory, where a throne awaited him, and where the Cardinals made their act of homage, kissing his ring and foot. Patriarchs and bishops followed suit. The Pope was then reminded of the mortality of all men, as he again sat on his Chair of State, while a Master of Ceremonies lit a piece of tow attached to a silver rod, then knelt before him and chanted in slow measure: "Holy Father! So passes the glory of the world." This warning was repeated when the Pope passed the bronze statue of St. Peter, of which only the dark, bearded metal face was to be seen, the body dressed in pontifical cope, the head crowned with a triple tiara—the two hundred and sixty-second Pope passing the effigy of the first. Then Mass began. Certain impressions linger in one's memory : the white-mitred figure, erect on its white throne in the apse with a flood of light upon it ; moments of absolute silence when one was conscious of the great sea of faces in the nave and transepts all bent in one direction ; a cloud of incense rising between the pillars of the great canopy above the altar where the Pope himself was officiating. There was the sudden thrill when his gentle voice was first heard, diffused by the loud-speakers throughout the building, as he intoned the *Gloria in Excelsis;* and the still greater thrill when silver trumpets, concealed in the dome, sounded triumphantly at the elevation of the Host.

Among the tens of thousands of every race and tongue crowding the Basilica, the royal stand assembled the delegations sent by more than fifty States : from the Crown Prince of Italy, in general's uniform, to the Irish Prime Minister, Mr. de Valera, in evening dress, with the broad ribbon of a Grand Cross over his chest ; from President Roosevelt's special ambassador, Mr. Joseph Kennedy, to the Duke of Norfolk, in knee breeches and garter, representing King George VI.

After five hours of pageantry inside the Basilica, the scene moved to the outer loggia of

St. Peter's.   More than half a million people had waited there from dawn, and it was now well past one. The ceremony can have had no equal in the annals of the Church. The eyes of the whole world were turned to it, the ears of the whole world tuned in to it through nation-wide broadcasts in both hemispheres, as Eugenio Pacelli sat on his throne, facing Rome and the world, surrounded by his court and his Cardinals, saluted by more than fifty princes of royal blood and distinguished statesmen who had come from all parts of the earth to honour him.   Before him the immense circle of St. Peter's Square enclosed within the Vatican colonnades, and the whole of the broad avenue, as far as the Tiber, packed with a solid mass of people.   The enormous crowd swayed and eddied, calling for him, waving handkerchiefs, cheering him.   Thus in full sight of the multitude the jewel bedecked golden tiara was placed on his head, and modern loud-speakers intoned, whilst modern wireless echoed into the farthest corners of the world, the time-honoured formula for the Coronation of a Pontiff : " Receive this Tiara of Three Crowns and know that you are the Father of Princes and Kings, the Governor of the Earth, the Vicar of our Saviour Jesus Christ."

XII

THE POPE AT WORK

As Secretary of State, the new Pope has already lived for the last nine years in the Vatican City. From that tiny territory—barely a hundred acres in size—some 350 million Catholics, spread all over the world, are governed spiritually. On this hill near the river Tiber the wicked Emperor Caligula once built a circus, where the early Christians were thrown to the lions and where St. Peter, first Bishop of Rome, was crucified head down. Three centuries later the first Christian Emperor, Constantine, built on the same spot a Basilica dedicated to St. Peter, the forerunner of the present Basilica. To the casual sightseer the Vatican, which for the last six centuries has been the principal residence of the Popes, is a city of palaces full of medieval pomp and renaissance splendour. But beneath all that sumptuousness the arduous and complex work of governing the world's greatest religious empire goes on. In his suite of rooms, immediately underneath the Papal flat, Cardinal Pacelli conducted during all those years the Vatican's official diplomatic relations with the Ambassadors and Ministers of some forty States accredited to the Holy See.

Pope Pius XII, ever since overcoming the frailty of his youth, has been blessed with good health. He has a strong heart and a sound constitution, he lives frugally and is a non-smoker (instead, so he tells friends, he gets his palliative out of assiduous newspaper reading; the principal papers in the languages which he has mastered are left with him every evening.) That he does not get easily tired he attributes to a concentrated and organized method of working. On the morning after his election he picked up the telephone on his desk at the usual hour, to tell his secretary that he was waiting.

A Pope is no doubt the hardest worked person in the world, with a daily routine more severe than that of a head of State and head of Government combined. For the Holy See is an autocracy. The whole enormous organization of the Church centres round the Pope, who wields complete authority and has the final word in everything, being accountable to no one.

THE POPE AT WORK

In the central organization of the Church the so-called Sacred Congregations are what the Departments of State are in the administration of a country. The Pope himself is Prefect (head) of three : the Supreme Congregation ; the Consistorial Congregation ; and that of the Oriental Church. Cardinals, mostly, head the other nine Congregations : the Sacramental Congregation ; that of the Council ; of the Religious Orders ; of the Propagation of the Faith (controlling all missionary activities) ; of the Rites ; of Seminaries and Universities ; and finally the Congregaton of the Fabric of St. Peter's. There are three Tribunals : the Apostolic Penitentiary, the Segnatura, and the Roman Rota. Apart from these administrative and judicial divisions there is the executive side of Church organization, the six administrative offices : the Chancellery ; the Datary ; the Secretariate of State ; the Apostolic Chamber ; the Secretariate for Briefs to Princes, and the Secretariate for Latin Letters. They all enjoy a certain measure of autonomy, but the Pope determines their policy and supervises their work. Spread over the week, he receives every day one of the heads to hear their report and guide their plans.

A large part of a Pope's day is reserved for

audiences. Each of the 1,200 Archbishops and Bishops of the Catholic Church is obliged to visit Rome once every five years, the canonical *ad limina* visit. This, in practice, means that there is one such important visitor almost every day for whom the Pope has to prepare by reading up previous reports so as to familiarize himself with the situation of his visitor's diocese. Then there are private audiences of distinguished personalities, arranged generally through their legations. Most of his time, however, is taken up by group audiences of pilgrims who have come from near and far to see the Pontiff, to kiss his ring, and to hear a fatherly word from his lips. Pius XII has broken with many traditions; he moves freely among his visitors, and these functions have nothing of the rigidity which both his predecessor's age and temperament had imposed. Religious functions at which he has to appear as the central figure are another heavy toll on his time and on his physique. As the Pope's daily consultation with his Secretary of State—reviewing the affairs of the world and the Church in general—takes already a couple of hours every morning, one can easily calculate that it is not until the afternoon is well gone that the Pope can settle down to undisturbed study.

THE POPE AT WORK

A walk in the Vatican gardens or in those of the Vatican Villa in the Alban Hills, is all the leisure which he can afford. For his responsibility and dignity never leave him; he cannot delegate them and has to carry their weight unto the grave.

The fact that he ascended the throne at an age below the average of his predecessors gives Pius XII a good expectation for a fruitful reign, an expectation heightened by the secret of his influence, the magnetism of his personality. His bearing, his manners—mirror of his temperament and judgment—are of a calm dignity. He has an air of abiding tranquillity; in fact in this serenity, paradoxical though it seems, there is something of utter worldliness. He is that rarest of combinations, a mystic and yet at the same time a practical man of action. Henry Bordeaux, the French Academician, once aptly described him as an El Greco portrait come to life.

That alone stamps him as the man for the task in hand, for never was a Pontiff elected in more anxious times, amidst the menacingly growing rumours of the war which was to break out barely six months later; amidst social, economic and political upheavals on a scale vaster than the world has witnessed ever before. In that clash

of ideas and ambitions he is not the champion of
any political ideology. When the democratic
countries hailed his election, just as, before, the
totalitarian countries had fulminated against its
possibility, it was not because Pacelli is a
democrat in the narrow sense of the word, but
because he has realised that totalitarianism with
its deification of temporary rulers, with its
ever-growing claim on the conscience and soul
of every citizen, makes complete liberty of
conscience impossible.

When he denounced Communism as the
world's greatest evil, he did so because in wiping
out the individuality of the family it destroys
society. With it he bracketed Nazism in the
same breath, for it strikes, no less ruthlessly, at
the individuality of the home, the very heart of
religion. Both are tyrannically pagan. The
Pope could never have exerted his influence to
stop Hitler at the cost of aiding Russia. His
endeavour goes out to stem left wing influence in
Fascism, which in itself has never been anti-
religious. Hence his influence on Franco to keep
Spain a Christian bulwark by following the model
of that most enlightened and beneficial of all
dictatorships : Salazar's Corporate State in
Portugal. Most revealing was his choice for

Secretary of State—his closest collaborator—of Cardinal Maglione, whose liberal inclinations are known from his long years as Nuncio in Paris, where, amongst others, he was the friend of Aristide Briand, that great European.

Pius XII shares to the full the human and courageous sentiments of Pius XI against all claims of the State to dominate the conscience of the individual, and against doctrines of racial persecution. He sees his "terrible responsibility," as he has called it, in the first place as an exhortation for peace between all nations—a peace based on "brotherly and reciprocal help, on friendly collaboration and cordial understanding," as he announced in his first allocution as Pope. That task he has taken up without shrinking. A year before, in Budapest, during a spell of acute tension and dread anticipation of a German conflict with Czecho-Slovakia, he quoted his predecessor as having said : " I thank God day by day that He has made me live in this time. This deep, all pervading crisis is unique in the history of mankind. One must be proud to be able to play one's part in this tremendous drama. Good and evil are interlocked in a gigantic struggle. Nobody has the right to be an onlooker at this momentous hour."

Six months later, on becoming Pope, he selected as his coat-of-arms a dove holding an olive branch in his beak, with as device " Opus Justitiae Pax " : The Work of Justice is Peace.

XIII

" THE WORK OF JUSTICE IS PEACE "

AFTER Pope Pius XII was crowned, international tension, which had been rampant all winter, began to move towards its inevitable spontaneous combustion.

The Pope worked incessantly through all these months, almost to the point of " neglecting his other duties," as he put it pathetically, supporting every effort that could have averted war. Even during what was to have been his summer holiday at Castel Gandolfo, he received day by day Ambassadors and Ministers of the powers accredited to him, as he called to him his own Nuncios from foreign capitals. The inside story of these papal efforts can, obviously, only be known to the statesmen immediately concerned ; it cannot be written until the momentous days of August, 1939, have definitely passed into history. At the last moment the Pope suddenly decided to enlist the moral support of public

G

opinion throughout the world by a personal broadcast, in which he stated clearly both the danger as well as his aim. Let us quote his own words, considered so historic that they have been reprinted verbatim in the British White Paper relating to the outbreak of hostilities :

" Once again a critical hour strikes for the great human family ; an hour of tremendous deliberations, towards which our hearts cannot be indifferent and from which our spiritual authority, which comes to us from God to lead souls in the ways of justice and of peace, must not hold itself aloof.

" Behold Us then with all of you, who in this moment are carrying the burden of so great a responsibility, in order that through Our voice you may hear the voice of that Christ from Whom the world received the most exalted example of living and in Whom millions and millions of souls repose their trust, in a crisis in which His word alone is capable of mastering all the tumultuous disturbances of the earth.

" Behold Us with you, leaders of peoples, men of state and men of arms, writers, orators and all those others who have the power to influence the thought and action of their fellow-men for whose destiny they are responsible.

94

"JUSTICE IS PEACE"

" We, armed only with the word of Truth and standing above all public disputes and passions, speak to you. To-day, notwithstanding Our repeated exhortations, the fear of bloody international conflict becomes more excruciating ; to-day when the tension of minds seems to have arrived at such a pass as to make the outbreak of the awful scourge of war appears imminent, We direct with paternal feeling a new and more heartfelt appeal to those in power and to their peoples ; to the former that, laying aside accusations, threats, causes of mutual distrust, they may attempt to resolve their present differences with the sole means suitable thereto, namely by reciprocal and trusting agreements ; to the latter that, in calm tranquillity, without disordered agitation, they may encourage the peaceful efforts of those who govern them.

" It is by force of reason and not by force of arms that justice makes progress ; and empires which are not founded on justice are not blessed by God. Statesmanship emancipated from morality betrays those very ones who would have it so. The danger is imminent but there is yet time. Nothing is lost with peace ; all may be with war. Let men return to mutual understanding. Let them begin negotiations anew.

Conferring with good will and with respect for reciprocal rights, they will find that to sincere and conscientious negotiators an honourable solution is never precluded.

" They will feel a sense of greatness—in the true sense of the word—if by silencing the voices of passion, be it collective or private, and by leaving to reason its rightful rule, they will have spared the blood of their fellow-men and saved their country from ruin.

" May the Almighty grant that the voice of this Father of the Christian family, of this Servant of servants who bears amongst them, unworthily, indeed, but nevertheless really, the person, the voice and the authority of Jesus Christ, find in the minds and in the hearts of men a ready and willing reception.

" May the strong hear Us that they may not become weak through injustice, may the powerful hear Us if they desire that their power be not destruction but rather a protection for their peoples and a safeguard to tranquillity in public order and in labour.

" We have with Us the hearts of mothers which beat as one with Ours ; the fathers who would be obliged to abandon their families ; the lowly who labour and do not understand ; the innocent upon whom weighs heavily the awful threat; the young men, generous with the purest and noblest ideas.

"And with Us all humanity seeks justice, bread, freedom; not steel which kills and destroys. With Us that Christ Who has made His one, solemn commandment—Love of one's brother—the very substance of His Religion and the promise of salvation for individuals and for nations. . . ."

Thus at the most crucial hour of " this ancient Europe " the Pope spoke as the supreme guardian of its Christian culture, and his words were listened to the whole world over. In a broadcast by Viscount Halifax later that same evening, the British Foreign Secretary referred twice in moving support to the Papal appeal. Premier Daladier issued at once an official statement, thanking the Holy Father, in the name of France, for his great effort with which he declared himself in complete agreement. The French Ambassador to the Vatican, M. Charles Roux; the Polish Ambassador, Dr. Papee; and the British Minister, Mr. d'Arcy Osborne, had had repeated conversations during these last days with the Pope and the Secretary of State. His endeavours proved of as little avail as the last minute appeals of the Queen of the Netherlands and the King of the Belgians, or that of Signor Mussolini.

One great moral result, however, rewarded the Pope's outspokenness. His broadcast opened the eyes of the Italian people. The man-in-the-street realized for the first time the yawning chasm which threatened to open in front of him. Great crowds had gathered round public loud-speakers ; and all cafés, shops and other public places had switched on to the Vatican wave-length. The way in which the broadcast—which came over perfectly everywhere—was received by the Italian people had the effect of a spontaneous plebiscite for peace.

The Pope's duty as Supreme Pastor being naturally directed to the salvation of souls, he has little to do with purely temporal contro-versies and territorial disputes between states. Only when great principles are involved does he speak out. Thus he could console Poland "which has earned the right of generous and fraternal sympathy of the world, to await the hour of a resurrection." Just as he uttered a grave warning to all Christendom, when he ceremonially received the credentials of the new Lithuanian Envoy to the Holy See, pointing out the "immeasurable dangers for the salvation of souls when, over the face of Europe which is Christian right down to its foundations, the dark shadow of the thought and work of the enemies of God is growing longer, closer and more menacing every day. In such circumstances, more than at any other period of its history, the preservation and the defence of Our Christian heritage take on a decisive importance for the future destiny of Europe and of each of its peoples, great or small."

All the admonitions and prayers of these eventful first months of his reign are crystallized in his first Encyclical, *Summi Pontificatus,* issued to the Archbishops and Bishops of the world on the eve of the Feast of Christ the King, at the end of October, 1939.

Being the programme of his Pontificate it is an engrossing document, as closely argued as it is outspoken. Renewing in plain language the denunciations by his predecessor, Pope Pius XII lashes out against " the error which pretends to absolve the civil authority from any dependence whatever on the Supreme Being, making it the primary cause and the absolute master of man, of society, and of all ties with the transcendent law deriving from God as its first source."

The success built on these falsehoods might
dazzle and bewilder simple folk for a time, but
the day of reckoning always comes, prophesies
the Pope :

" It is quite true that power based on such
weakness and on such an unsteady foundation
can attain at times, under certain circumstances,
material successes which are apt to arouse
wonder in superficial observers ; but the moment
comes when the inevitable law triumphs, striking'
down all that has been constructed on a hidden
or open disproportion between the greatness of
the material or outward success and the weakness of the inner values and moral foundations."

And thinking of the suffering and fears of
countless parents, those innumerable afflictions
" of which no statistics are able to speak," he
warns the State that it can go no further, for
" the more burdensome become the material
sacrifices demanded by the State of individuals
and of families, the more sacred and inviolable
too must be the rights of their consciences.
Goods, blood it can demand, but the souls
redeemed by God, never. . . ."

From his exalted and impartial observation
post the Pope then scrutinizes the international
scene. He castigates the world's departure from

the basic principles of international morality, as the source of the present war. " These principles demand respect for the rights of every nation to independence, to life and to the possibility of progressive evolution in the ways of civilization. They demand, also, faithfulness to stipulated and sanctioned treaties in conformity with the principles of the rights of man. . . . There is no doubt," continues the Encyclical, " that the preliminary and necessary condition of all common, pacific life between the nations, the very soul of juridical relations between them, is to be found in mutual trust, in the expectation and conviction of respect for the plighted word. But to consider in principle that treaties are ephemeral, and to take upon oneself the tacit authority to rescind them unilaterally on the day that they are no longer convenient, means the destruction of all reciprocal confidence between the nations. Natural order would be thrown into chaos ; trenches of division, impossible to overcome, would be dug between the peoples and the nations. . . . These are the conceptions which have brought the world to the present horrible abyss. . . ."

From the gloom of the moment, the Statesman

looks forward to the peace to come, to the new order which is to safeguard Europe from repeated destruction. It must not be, so the Pope warns, a repetition of past mistakes, an inhuman *Vae Victis*. And here the Democracies, responsible for the disastrous Peace Treaties after the last war, are set to search their conscience : " What will be the future order when the tempest of war shall have ceased ?   Will there be a repetition of the past mistakes which put the right of the victor above every sense of justice ? No, safety cannot come from the sword.   It can impose peace, but it cannot create peace. . . ."

To attain that great aim the Pope calls for a spiritual re-education and for religious regeneration. For " the profound and ultimate root of the present evils is the refusal to accept a standard of universal morality in the life of the individual, in social life and in international relations ; that is disregard and forgetfulness of the natural law whose foundation is in God. When God is denied every basis of morality is undermined. The much vaunted laicisation of society had caused the reappearance of signs of a corrupt and corrupting paganism in regions where for centuries Christian civilization had shone."

Finally, with a ringing admonition for a spirit which he already sees in every region of the Catholic world, to face boldly, in close collaboration between clergy and laity, the gigantic task of our age, the Pope closes his first Pastoral Letter.

Having denounced that armed heresy, racialism, in a sentence of classic beauty, recalling that " human solidarity and charity which is dictated by our common origin and by the sacrifice of Christ's redemption," the Supreme Pontiff, immediately after his return to his capital, consecrated with his own hands before the High Altar of St Peter's four coloured Bishops—a Hindu, a Chinese, a Negro, and a native of Madagascar—his Venerable Brethren.

Thus, in this turbulent world of ours, Pope Pius XII, loyal to the clear and single-minded purpose of his whole career, will use all his enormous influence, all his unsurpassed gifts of head and heart, to be verily the " Pontifex Maximus," his supreme title which, literally translated, means " *the* Builder of Bridges."

Behind him he has his unique position as Head of the Catholic Church—now numbering 350 million adherents—the greatest power on earth

that ever was, is, or will be, as two hundred and
sixty-second Pope of Rome. What that means,
the greatest English historian, and a Protestant
at that, a hundred years ago described in an
essay which has become classic, for it is true to
this day. To quote Lord Macaulay :

'' There is not, and there never was on this
earth, a work of human policy so well deserving
of examination as the Roman Catholic Church.
The history of that Church joins together the
two great ages of human civilization. No other
institution is left standing which carries the mind
back to the times when the smoke of sacrifice
rose from the Pantheon and when camelopards
and tigers bounded in the Flavian amphitheatre.
The proudest royal houses are but of yesterday,
when compared with the line of the Supreme
Pontiffs. That line we trace back in an
unbroken series, from the Pope who crowned
Napoleon in the nineteenth century to the Pope
who crowned Pepin in the eighth ; and far beyond
the time of Pepin the august dynasty extends,
till it is lost in the twilight of fable. The republic
of Venice came next in antiquity. But it was
modern when compared with the Papacy ; and
it is gone and the Papacy remains. The Papacy
remains, not in decay, not a mere antique, but

full of life and youthful vigour. The Catholic
Church is still sending forth to the farthest ends
of the world missionaries as zealous as those who
landed in Kent with Augustine, and still con-
fronting hostile kings with the same spirit with
which she confronted Attila. The number of her
children is greater than in any former age. Her
acquisitions in the New World have more than
compensated for what she has lost in the Old.
Her spiritual ascendancy extends over the vast
countries which lie between the plains of the
Missouri and Cape Horn, countries which, a
century hence, may not improbably contain a
population as large as that which now inhabits
Europe. The members of her communion are
certainly not fewer than those of all other
Christian sects united. Nor do we see any sign
which indicates that the term of her long
dominion is approaching. She saw the
commencement of all the ecclesiastical estab-
lishments that now exist in the world ; and we
feel no assurance that she is not destined to see
the end of them all. She was great and
respected before the Saxon had set foot on
Britain, before the Frank had passed the Rhine,
when Grecian eloquence still flourished at
Antioch, when idols were still worshipped in the

temple of Mecca. She shall still exist when some traveller from New Zealand may, in the midst of a vast solitude, take his stand on a broken arch of London Bridge to sketch the ruins of St. Paul's.''